HISTORIC ST. AUGUSTINE

HISTORIC LANDMARKS

Jason Cooper

The Rourke Book Company, Inc.
Vero Beach, Florida 32964

© 2001 The Rourke Book Company, Inc.

All rights reserved. No part of this book may be reproduced or utilized in any form or by any means, electronic or mechanical including photocopying, recording, or by any information storage and retrieval system without permission in writing from the publisher.

PHOTO CREDITS:
All photos © Lynn M. Stone

PRODUCED & DESIGNED by East Coast Studios
eastcoaststudios.com

EDITORIAL SERVICES:
Janice L. Smith for Penworthy Learning Systems

Library of Congress Cataloging-in-Publication Data

Cooper, Jason, 1942-
   Historic St. Augustine / Jason Cooper.
     p. cm. — (Historic Landmarks)
   Includes index.
   ISBN 1-55916-328-3
   1. Historic Sites—Florida—Saint Augustine—Juvenile literature. 2. Saint Augustine (Fla.)—History—Juvenile literature. [1. Saint Augustine (Fla.)—History. 2. Historic sites.] I. Title II. Series.

F319.S2 C66 2000
975.9'18—dc21
                                                  00–038728

Printed in the USA

TABLE OF CONTENTS

St. Augustine	5
Old St. Augustine	9
Visiting St. Augustine	20
Glossary	23
Index	24
Further Reading	24

ST. AUGUSTINE

Long before Florida had a Miami, Fort Myers, or Orlando, it had St. Augustine.

St. Augustine is almost older than Florida oranges. Curiously, a man named Juan Ponce de Leon had something to do with both the **citrus** (SIH trus) and the city.

Ponce de Leon was a Spanish explorer and gold seeker. His ship stopped somewhere along Florida's northeast coast in 1513.

St. Augustine was a birthplace of Florida and U.S. history. Ponce de Leon's landing near here in 1513 began a parade of tourists that has yet to stop.

Ponce de Leon and his men no doubt brought oranges with them from Spain. The seeds of those oranges became Florida's first orange trees. More important, Ponce de Leon began Spain's interest in Florida.

By 1565, Don Pedro Menendez had been sent to Florida from Spain to set up a post for soldiers. That **military** (MIL uh ter ee) post was not far from where Ponce de Leon had landed in 1513.

The post became St. Augustine. And St. Augustine thus became the oldest city in America permanently settled by Europeans.

Visitors listen to a National Park Service ranger in an old Spanish uniform.

OLD ST. AUGUSTINE

St. Augustine has had a long and colorful history. Six different flags, beginning with Spain's, have flown over the city.

Spain's grip on Florida and St. Augustine was always shaky. France, England, and finally, the United States, wanted Florida, too.

Attacks on St. Augustine by pirates and British soldiers caused Spain to build 2 rock forts. The larger was Castillo de San Marcos. It was built on the edge of St. Augustine. The Castillo remains there today, looking very much like it did 3 centuries ago.

Old guns on the upper walls of the Castillo point toward the ocean's inlet at St. Augustine.

The second fort, Matanzas, was much smaller. It was built 14 miles (22 kilometers) south of the city overlooking Matanzas Inlet and the Matanzas River. Like the Castillo, Fort Matanzas remains in good condition. Both forts are national monuments, looked after by the National Park Service.

Castillo de San Marcos was at the center of more than 200 years of St. Augustine's history. Building of the fort began in 1672. It was not finished until 1695. The fort was never taken by force. But like all of Florida, St. Augustine and her Castillo changed ownership several times.

Fort Matanzas, south of St. Augustine, is much smaller than the castillo. Matanzas defended the "back door" waterway to St. Augustine.

Old buildings, like this wooden schoolhouse, give visitors to St. Augustine's old, narrow streets plenty to visit.

An artist working outdoors on historic St. George Street paints a historic St. Augustine building.

A **treaty** (TREE tee), or agreement, between Spain and Great Britain in 1763 turned Florida over to the British. St. Augustine became the capital of East Florida.

Another treaty returned Florida to Spain in 1784. Spain's second rule in Florida ended in 1821. Rather than risk war with the United States, Spain handed Florida to the U.S. for almost nothing. The Castillo was renamed Fort Marion.

The old Spanish forts had great waterfront views, but the comforts for soldiers—or prisoners—were few.

The U.S. used the fort as a prison and as part of its coast defense. The famous Seminole warrior Osecola was jailed there.

Florida became a state in 1845. In 1860 Florida joined other Southern states in the Confederate States of America. Fort Marion became a Confederate fort in 1861. A fifth flag flew over St. Augustine.

The Gonzalez-Alvarez house is the oldest house in St. Augustine. It dates back to the early 1700s.

After the start of the Civil War (1861), a U.S. Navy warship retook the fort and the city without firing a shot.

After the war, the fort was used as a prison, most often for army **deserters** (di ZERT erz) and Indians. The fort had no value as a defense against modern weapons. In 1924 it became a national monument.

A horse-drawn buggy passes the old Tovar house. Five of the six flags that have flown over St. Augustine (basically the same U.S. flag has flown twice) wave from the deck.

VISITING ST. AUGUSTINE

St. Augustine has kept many of its ties to the past. The heart of downtown St. Augustine has dozens of old buildings on narrow streets like King and St. George. The city's oldest surviving house was built about 1706. The Basilica Cathedral of St. Augustine includes a church **parish** (PAIR ish) built in 1797.

The National Park Service runs a ferry boat to Fort Matanzas. And Castillo de San Marcos is an easy walk from downtown St. Augustine.

Henry Flagler's amazing Ponce de Leon Hotel is now Flagler College.

In more recent years, St. Augustine was a grand winter resort. The rich and famous followed the footsteps—and rails—of Henry Flagler. Flagler built the magnificent, 540-room Ponce de Leon Hotel here in 1885. He also built the Florida East Coast Railroad, which brought guests to his hotel.

The hotel is now Flagler College. The Florida East Coast Railroad is gone, but Amtrak® passenger trains still rumble into St. Augustine.

GLOSSARY

citrus (SIH trus) — a related group of trees that produce pulpy, juicy fruit with thick skins; the grapefruit and orange family

deserter (di ZERT er) — one who leaves without permission

military (MIL uh ter ee) — referring to a country's armed forces and their weapons

parish (PAIR ish) — a church community

treaty (TREE tee) — an official agreement between nations, often used to end warfare

INDEX

Castillo de San Marcos   9, 11, 14, 20
Civil War   19
Confederate States of America   16
Europeans   6
Flagler, Henry   22
flags   9, 16
Florida   5, 6, 9, 11, 14, 16
Florida East Coast Railroad   22
Fort Marion   14, 16
Fort Matanzas   11, 20
Great Britain   14
Menendez, Don Pedro   6
National Park Service   11, 20
Ponce de Leon, Juan   5, 6
prison   19
St. Augustine   5, 6, 9, 11, 14, 20, 22
Spain   6, 9, 14
United States   9, 14, 16

FURTHER READING

Find out more about St. Augustine and the Castillo de San Marcos with these helpful books and information sites:

Ashbranner, Brent K. *A Strange and Distant Shore: Indians of the Great Plains in Exile.* Penguin Putnam, 1996.

Wills, Charles A. *A Historical Album of Florida.* Millbrook, 1994.

Castillo de San Marcos National Monument
   www.nps.gov/casa
St. Augustine History
   st.johns.k12fl.us/history